Songcraft

Exploring the Art of Christian Songwriting

Revised and Updated

What others are saying about Songcraft

"Songwriting is a craft that must be learned. Matt's book will be helpful to anybody looking to hone their skills as they seek to grow in this gifting".
Al Gordon – songwriter and worship leader
Worship Central, UK

"From getting to know Matt and working with him through Homegrown Worship, he is a devoted follower of Jesus who is a deep, well-considered thinker with a passion for exploring truth and theology in his songwriting. I'm sure many people will find this book useful as they explore their own songwriting journey."
Nick Law – songwriter, worship leader, Chief Song Selector
Homegrown Worship, UK

"Enjoy learning about music/song writing from a man with diverse culture. This book will help inspire the song writer in you, as you are reminded God gave the gift and learn how to use it for His glory."
Michal Maddix-Hayford – songwriter and worship leader, UK

"Matt writes with the heart of a pastor and the aching feet of a journeyed songwriter, inviting others to join him on the road. His blend of personal stories and practical tips is both inviting and accessible. And his encouragement to pursue God before all else rings loudest of all."

Joel Payne – songwriter, worship leader
RESOUNDworship, UK

"Earthed in his own experience and packed with helpful advice Matt has written a book that demystifies the process of songwriting.

With a down to-earth, approach he guides the reader through the nuts and bolts of creating a congregational song whilst clearly identifying the need for worship to be both the source and the goal of our compositions.

I'm sure it will prove to be a valuable resource to aspiring and seasoned writers alike."

Dave Bilbrough -songwriter and worship leader, UK

"A journey through the simplicity and complexity of the art of song writing, with relatable tales and mind-blowing insight. This book is truly better than a lot of books we've read on the subject. All songwriters who want to bring the Kingdom on earth must read this book!"

Tommy & Joany Deuschle – songwriters and worship leaders
Celebration Church, Zimbabwe

"Songcraft is a wonderful toolkit for Christian songwriters who want to develop their skills in the art of songwriting, especially those who desire to write congregational-friendly songs. It's practical, thorough and easy to understand. While it reminded me of many of the current techniques I use in crafting my songs, I learned some very helpful tips which I know will help me to improve and continue to grow as a writer. Whether you're a novice or have been crafting songs for years, this book will really empower you in your gift."

Loulita Gill – songwriter and worship leader, UK

Songcraft

Exploring the Art of Christian Songwriting

Revised and Updated

Matt McChlery

FAITHSEED
BOOKS

SONGCRAFT: Exploring the Art of Christian Songwriting (Revised and Updated)
Copyright © Matt McChlery 2021
www.mattmcchlery.com

Matt McChlery has asserted his rights under the Copyright, Design and Patents Act 1988 to be identified as the Author of this Work.

All rights reserved.
No part of this publication may be reproduced, stored in a retrieval system, or transmitted, in any form or by any means, without the prior permission in writing of the publisher, nor be otherwise circulated in any form of binding or cover other than that in which it is published and without a similar condition including this condition being imposed on the subsequent purchaser.

First Published © Matt McChlery 2010 under the title *Songcraft: Exploring the art of Song Writing* by Matt McChlery. Second Edition Published in 2020. This Third Edition Published in 2021 by Faithseed Books (an imprint of Matt McChlery Ministries), 34 Windsor Drive, Wisbech, PE13 3HJ, United Kingdom.

ISBN: 978-1-7398024-0-0

Cover photos © 2019 Shravan Sharma. Cover design © 2020 Ryan Baker-Barnes.

Unless otherwise indicated, biblical quotations are from the HOLY BIBLE, NEW INTERNATIONAL VERSION ®. Copyright © 1973, 1978, 1984 by International Bible Society. Used by permission of International Bible Society. Used by permission. Scripture quotations identified as The Message are from THE MESSAGE. Copyright © 1993, 1994, 1995, 1996, 200, 2001, 2002. Used by permission of NavPress Publishing Group. Used by permission. Scripture quotations identified as NKJV are from THE HOLY BIBLE, NEW KING JAMES VERSION. Copyright © 1982 by Thomas Nelson, Inc. Used by permission.

For my Mum, Dad and sister Leigh
Thanks for your continued encouragement, support and love.

Contents

Foreword 13

Introduction 15

Chapter 1: The Songwriter's Toolkit 17

Chapter 2: Inspiration 25

Chapter 3: Basic Ingredients 43

Chapter 4: Questions to ask Yourself 53

Chapter 5: Practical Tips 71

Chapter 6: Cultural Relevance 85

Chapter 7: Sharing Your Song 93

Chapter 8: The Power of Words 103

Chapter 9: Live Your Song	111
Chapter 10: And Finally	117
Useful Websites	119
Thanks	127
About the Author	129
Let's Get Writing	133

Foreword

Christian music has a storeroom of new and old treasures. The gifted musician knows the value of this heritage and then adds their own unique voice to this growing wealth.

Matt McChlery follows in such a tradition. His great, great, great-grandfather composed 'Onward Christian Soldiers'; generations later his songs speak those same truths but with the impact of the sound for today.

Matt has been involved in the music of churches for many years, leading worship at various events as well as speaking about worship and songwriting. Since moving to the UK in 2003, Matt has been developing a ministry in music. He leads the music of

Songcraft

The King's Church in Wisbech often adding his own original compositions that help reflect the journey of our church, as well as turning the hearts of those singing his words, to God. He also seeks to inspire and nurture those who dedicate their ability for God's glory and has begun a song writing workshop with members of the congregation.

In these pages Matt examines the process of seeking to express in song that which is beyond the measure of words and melody. In doing so, he draws on the ability granted to him, often gleaned from others, in the hope that you will find inspiration to add your voice to the song that never ends.

Clive Butcher

The King's Church, Wisbech - UK

Introduction

At the tender age of thirteen, I gave my life to Jesus at a Christian rock concert. I did not know it then, but music and songwriting were to play an ever-increasing role in my life.

By the age of fifteen, after teaching myself to play the guitar (with a little help along the way), I found myself standing in front of around two hundred of my peers on my own, guitar in hand, leading them in praise and worship. My journey had begun.

From then on I guess you could say I was passionate about worship and I started writing songs. Looking back on some of my earlier attempts, it is truly embarrassing to see my infantile efforts, yet at the same time very humbling to see where God has taken me. Although I may be embarrassed about them, those songs I wrote in the early years were vitally important. They were the first baby-steps along my journey, a journey where walking with God and being willing to grow and learn were vitally important. Indeed, a journey I am still walking today.

I do not claim to know all the answers about the elusive art of songwriting. I recognise that I too have still got a lot to learn. So please don't see me as a song writing guru, but rather a fellow traveller who has a few tips and advice to offer, that you have met along the way.

I hope that this book feeds your creativity and encourages you to keep on going! (This path we have chosen to travel is not an easy one). As you peruse its pages and dwell on its words, I hope new songs are birthed in your spirit, and when you are done, you are ready once again to take your next step along this wonderful journey of songwriting.

Matt McChlery

CHAPTER ONE

The Songwriter's Toolkit

Before climbing a mountain, it is always a good idea to go to the outdoor activity shop at the mall and make sure you have got all the equipment you need in order to make the expedition safe and successful.

Likewise, when writing a song, there are several bits of kit that I have found extremely useful and wouldn't write a song without!

When writing songs it is important to get your ideas down onto a piece of paper, or into a voice recorder as quickly as possible. I don't know about you, but I find it extremely difficult to remember certain melodies or lyrics shortly after singing them. I have to get them recorded in one form or another or risk losing them forever. In this chapter I will be making a few suggestions as to how ideas and sounds can be recorded quickly and easily. However, technology does change and not everyone has the same access to it, so you need to find what works best for you.

Songwriting Journal

Here is a form of technology that is unlikely to change soon and hopefully everyone has access to – pencil and paper!

When I first began writing songs I would write down my ideas on any scrap of paper that I had to hand at the time. Writing is a good way to record lyrical ideas quickly and easily. I have also adopted my own version of shorthand to help me get my ideas down even quicker. Ditto marks are also very useful. The only problem with writing songs and ideas onto lots of different pieces of paper is that they get lost! So I went out and bought myself a hard-backed exercise book that I've covered 'creatively'. I call it my 'Songwriting Journal'.

It's great to have a record of all your songwriting efforts in one place. It is encouraging when you are having a bad day and your creativity seems to have dried up, to look back over those ideas and songs that you *have* written. Also, it is handy to have past ideas at your fingertips to draw upon when you are writing. Sometimes a chorus from an unfinished song will fit perfectly with the new song you are working on.

I once spoke to an author who wrote fiction books. He had his writing draft manuscript with him and showed me part of his method. He would only write his actual text of the story on the right-hand page which left the left-hand page available for him to write revisions, add extra bits, jot down research etc. After speaking with him I adapted my method of writing my drafts of songs in my journal.

I too use the right-hand page for the actual lyrics of the song. The left-hand page is used to jot down key words, Bible verses, pieces of research, experiment with different lyrics or rhymes etc. Sometimes both pages end up with so much writing on them I have to turn over and use a clean sheet to write the final version of the song on.

Recording Devices

Another way to record your ideas, especially melodies, is on a recording device of some kind. In the early days I found using a Dictaphone an ideal songwriting tool. It was small, light and portable and very easy to use. It was perfect for recording spontaneous melodies that I just start humming while walking down the street, as well as recording my 'songwriting sessions' where I'm in the zone, playing my guitar and singing, just worshipping the Lord. It freed me up to stop worrying about missing any good ideas or phrases that may or may not arise.

As technology has developed and advanced I now increasingly use my mobile phone or tablet computer in the same way as I did the Dictaphone. There are several apps available that allow you to record voice memos. This means that wherever I am, I have a recording device I can use. Although, I have received some funny looks from people on the train when they see me singing into my phone.

Musical Instruments

Songwriters do not need to know how to play a musical instrument in order to write great songs. If you have a melody in your heart and some awesome words to go with it, you've got a song in the making. However, if you do know how to play an instrument, it does help.

For those who can't play, find a friend who does play an instrument to help you work out the notes and chords that make up your song. It would also be helpful if you try to learn a little bit about music, such as the names of the notes and how many beats are in the bar. This will help you communicate a lot more easily with those who are musical.

If you do play an instrument, try not to get too stuck in your ways. What I mean is, try to change the chords and chord sequences that you use to stop your songs from sounding too 'samey'. If you find that you are getting stuck in a rut, try to write away from your instrument for a while.

I'm often asked what comes first, the melody or the words? This is another difficult question to answer. I find it is a combination of things. It all goes back to what has happened to spark my creativity at that particular moment. Sometimes a word or phrase really excites me and I try to write a song around that idea. Other times I can just be playing my guitar and stumble across a different chord and the new sound leads me into wanting to use it in a song.

Dictionary and Thesaurus

It may seem obvious, but as we craft the lyrics to our songs, we are dealing with words, so it is important that we know exactly what those words mean. A dictionary will help with word meanings and definitions as well as spelling. A rhyming dictionary is not cheating. In fact, it is a very useful, sensible and time saving way of finding words that rhyme – especially if you are using a strict rhyme pattern in your song.

I love thesauruses. I have found them to be an invaluable songwriting tool. Very often I get stuck either because I do not want to use the same old words or cliché to explain something or I find I have already used the word 'good' in the first verse, so I need something different elsewhere. Thesauruses are a treasure trove of vocabulary and using one will help to make your vocabulary richer.

A Bible App

Bible apps are great as they contain so much information all in one place that can be accessed quickly and easily. When writing Christian songs having a Bible handy is a really good idea. Having different translations of the Bible help to shed new light on certain topics or give you a deeper insight into something that you are looking at. Often, I find one translation works better if used in a song than another, so having various options available is a good idea. Translations can easily be switched between on an app such as Bible Gateway or The Bible App (YouVersion).

Also searching for a specific theme within the Bible such as 'baptism' or 'slavery' could be done in an old-fashioned concordance. However, apps and search engines do help to make this process easier and quicker.

Music Theory

Writing songs is not limited only to those who know music theory just as much as it isn't restricted to those who can play an instrument. However, knowing some of the basics of music theory does help as you have a better understanding of how music works and what makes it work in the way that it does.

My basic knowledge of music theory was gained partly through the few years I attempted to learn the piano, from being part of a church choir at senior school where you had to know how to read sheet music as well as a music theory class I took at roughly the same time. My understanding only goes up to about a Grade 3 level (there are 8 Grades in total) so I don't transcribe, or write, the music myself. I use other tools and methods to help record the melody such as chord charts and audio recordings. However, for those songs that have made it to the studio recording stage and have been officially released, I have invested in getting a professional with more music theory knowledge than myself to transcribe the song as sheet music as I know that this is a method of reading and understanding music that is preferred by some musicians, rather than just having access to a chord chart.

Although having a notated piece of sheet music is not a necessary part of writing a song, music theory does need to be understood to some degree.

Songcraft

You will have a better grasp of time signatures and key signatures. You will have an idea as to which chords and therefore which notes you could use as part of a melody. It will be easier to identify the length of notes in a given melody and therefore help repetition or variation. Most importantly it will give you a bit of vocabulary to help you communicate your ideas a little more clearly with a band or a producer.

As my flurry into music theory was decades ago, I admit I have forgotten a lot of it. So, as a way of dipping in to remind myself of the odd thing or two I have bought a book about basic music theory called: 'Music Theory for Dummies'. I am sure there are many books available that give a few of the basics of music theory so you don't have to use the same one that I do.

You may feel you want to go one step further and take a music theory class. If you ask at your local college or a music teacher, they may be able to point you in the right direction. Alternatively, you could take an online course or watch some YouTube videos.

CHAPTER TWO

Inspiration

One question that I am asked most often is 'What inspired you to write that?' This is often an area that fascinates those who don't write songs and frustrates those who do. I am no exception! I sometimes feel that I spend more time being frustrated about not being inspired than I do actually writing songs - and even then, most of what I do write is no good.

Inspiration is very fluid. By this I mean that it is always moving, flowing, changing and is difficult to define in any specific way. You could say that inspiration is the spark that ignites a creative mind. But where does this spark come from? How can we go about finding it? Can we learn how to make this spark for ourselves or do we wait around for it to happen spontaneously?

The Source of Creativity

Most creative people have a muse that fuels their passion and desire to be creative. Some are inspired by their love for a certain person. Others may find inspiration in alcohol or drugs. There are some that feel passionately about a cause or ideal. And there are those who get captivated by an idea or image. What is your muse? Where is the source of your creativity?

As Christian songwriters, I hope that your answer will be 'Jesus'. Is Jesus your beginning and your end? Is He your love, your passion and desire? Is He your cause? Are you captivated by Him? Our songwriting needs to flow out of a deep relationship with God. It is only as God reveals himself to us that we can write about Him, for Him and to Him. There is no better source of creativity than *The Creator* Himself! "In the beginning God created the heavens and the earth" (Genesis 1:1 NIV). Just think about it, God created everything. He created you and He also created music and song. So, if you want to write songs why not draw from the eternal source of creativity?

The way to do this is summed up in one word: *relationship*. It is vital that we are in a living relationship with Jesus every day. This means actively pursuing His presence through regular prayer, worship, reading the Bible, going to church to meet with other believers, and living our lives according to His Word. This may all sound obvious, but it is important that we establish this because how can we write about someone we know nothing about?

Communication vs. Intimacy

A while ago, God revealed to me the difference between communication and intimacy. I had been going through a rough patch in the area of spending time with God on my own. As a result, I noticed that I was going through a creative 'dry season' and I was becoming extremely frustrated. So, I determined to start communicating with God again on a regular basis in order to get back in touch with Him. After a while of going through the motions of communication – rushing through a quick prayer, maybe singing a song or reading a few verses from the Bible – nothing was happening. I still felt as distant and uninspired as I had done before. I was not waiting on the Lord or being still and quiet. I had forgotten to stop and listen. It's the Mary and Martha scenario again.

God dropped this revelation into my spirit. During that season, God and I *were* communicating, but we were not being intimate. Prayer and worship are communication, but not necessarily times of intimacy. It's intimacy that God is after. I realised that my songwriting was in a dry season due to my lack of intimacy, not lack of communication. With intimacy comes strength, security and creativity. There is a greater depth, a stronger bond, a closer presence that only comes from intimacy with the King of kings and Lord of lords.

Our Talents are from Him

Our relationship with God is also important in that I believe He is the one who gives us our talents to use for His glory. The parable of the Talents in Matthew's Gospel[1], although it refers to money, helps to illustrate this point. Those servants who took the talents entrusted to them and invested in them were congratulated by the master and were given even more, "Well done, good and faithful servant! You have been faithful with a few things; I will put you in charge of many things. Come and share your master's happiness!"[2]. But the servant who hid the talents given to him because he was too afraid of failure was severely chastised.

He has entrusted us with His precious gifts to be a blessing to others as well as to give glory back to Him. If we are not in a relationship with Him we will not be able to receive His gifts with the right heart, nor use them in the right way.

---

[1] Matthew 25:14-30
[2] Matthew 25:23

Inspiration

When I was still in primary school, my mother made me attend piano lessons. I didn't enjoy them very much and was not particularly inspired by them, after all it was hard work and the practising was so cumbersome. One birthday I was given a nylon-stringed guitar. I thought it was pretty cool but had no idea how to play it, so it ended up living in the back of my cupboard for a few years. Until one day, someone suggested that I try to learn how to play the guitar. My piano teacher at the time also taught guitar, so off I went for my first lesson, full of excitement and anticipation. She tried to show me where to put my fingers and how to hold the instrument. I thought I was doing fine, until the time came for me to try to strum. It was a disaster! My teacher was so fed up with me that I remember her telling my mother and me not to bother to come back for another lesson because there was no way I would ever learn how to play the guitar in my life! As you can imagine, this crushed my spirit and the guitar went straight into the back of the cupboard again.

It was only some years later while I was at senior school, that one of the teachers who ran the Scripture Union there asked me if I had ever tried playing the guitar before. I was a brand-new Christian at the time. I told him about my bad experience, but despite this he encouraged me to give it another go. He showed me a few chords, wrote some simple chord charts and left me to it. Something began stirring within me. I kept practising every week and found that I enjoyed it so much I practised every moment I got. I was discovering new things about the instrument all on my own: the technique required; its different sounds - and it thrilled me. My ability grew and soon I could change between chords with no break in the beat. I got hold of some simple three-chord songs that we sung at the Scripture Union meetings and began to practise them. The end of the year came and the teacher who had introduced me to the guitar announced that he was leaving the school. Then the unthinkable happened. He asked me to take over leading the singing at the Scripture Union meetings! I had only been playing guitar for five months, knew how to play six chords, (but could only play three properly), and the next thing I knew I was standing in front of two hundred peers, all on my own, singing my heart out to the Lord!

I believe that it was God who enabled and equipped me with my gift of playing the guitar. I was useless before I knew Him, and now that I know Him, He has shown me how to play and has given me the ability with which to do it. Not only that, he has birthed a passion in me for writing songs, for singing, for leading, for teaching, for equipping, and for spreading worship of His name around the world. It is only through relationship that God has taken me further and helped me develop and fine-tune the gifts that He has given me.

When God gives us a gift or a talent, it is a very precious thing. It needs us to take hold of it, care for it, nurture it, invest in it and grow it into the thing that God intends it to be. Just like a seed, it needs to be cared for in order for it to flourish. As songwriters this means we need to do what we can to get better, have lessons, get training to play our instruments with better skill, or vocal coaching to help us sing better. Do not neglect the gift that is in you.

Being in Tune with The Spirit

"Since we live by the Spirit, let us keep in step with the Spirit"[3]. Our relationship with God also influences and affects how in tune we are with Him and what He is doing in the Spirit, on the earth, in our nation, in our community, in our church and in our lives. The level of our relationship determines the depth of our revelation. As songwriters, it is important that we are mindful of what God is doing in all aspects, so that we can follow Him and write songs that reflect this, therefore enabling others to engage with that same flow or move of the spirit.

---

[3] Galatians 5:25

Songcraft

In this instance, our relationship with God is vital for the songs we write to be anointed with His Spirit as well as being written with excellence. For a radio to work correctly it needs to be tuned in to the appropriate station, otherwise all you get is static. If the radio is not tuned, it doesn't mean that the signal is no longer there. Sometimes in our lives, it feels as if all we are receiving is static. We have received a bump which has moved our spiritual tuner out of place, and it seems as if God is no longer there. Just wait a moment. Take some time out to re-tune your spiritual receiver. God is still there, and He is longing to talk to you and sing over you.

Darlene Zschech puts it like this: "A songwriter could go to a hundred classes on how to write 'hit' songs, but the craft is only part of the writer's commission when it comes to bringing the sounds of heaven to earth. One doesn't accidentally write a heaven song. Songs that truly connect the spirit of man with his Creator will always be birthed through the well-worn path to the throne room of God, a path the writer has travelled to and from many times"[4].

---

[4] Darlene Zschech, Extravagant Worship, Bethany House 2001, 2002, p.191. Used by permission.

Inspiration

Crossword Puzzles and Lightning Bolts

I understand that all of us are individuals, created to be different from each other. This means that our preferred ways of song writing and the things that inspire us will all be different. There is beauty in diversity, so don't be discouraged if one particular style is not for you, you will have a style that is all your own - embrace it!

There are those who have mastered the discipline of writing. One friend of mine, Andrew Baird, who has written numerous number-one hits in Zimbabwe, tells me that he writes songs as a hobby. Just as some people enjoy doing a crossword or a sudoku in their spare time, he writes songs.

I find that the way I write is more likely to come as a sudden lightening bolt, a flash of inspiration that I have to grasp quickly and write it down before it vanishes! Although, I must say that I have sat down and just written a song like doing a crossword puzzle, but my more likely method is the lightning bolt.

I am sure for you too it will be a mixture of things. Recognise your preferred method, but don't discount the others. Perhaps just by trying something different will give you more inspiration.

All Dried Up

There are many times when I feel that my inspiration is all dried up. These are the times of frustration when I sit down, wanting to write and sing and be inspired, but nothing happens. No gems are unearthed in my spirit and no lightening bolts strike my heart. Due to my recognised trend of inspiration, I find that I need to find ways of stimulating my creativity. I need to actively seek out sparks of inspiration.

I try to unlock my creativity in many different ways, and I am constantly looking for new things to try. My first suggestion is to listen to other genres of music that you do not normally listen to. For example, I prefer soft rock, pop, worship and Christian contemporary music (CCM), so I have made it a point to try to listen to other types of music in order to hear as wide a range of sound as possible and see how melody and lyric is used in different ways. These other types of music include jazz, hip-hop, classical, gospel, indie, RnB, dance and African or world music. I believe it is important for Christian songwriters to listen to the new sounds that are current in the secular music world. Do not compromise on belief, as in, don't dwell on songs that are promoting promiscuity, drug taking or have lots of swearing. But there are lots of songs out there that do not fall into that category and are alright to listen to. It is extremely important for us to be in tune with The Spirit, as I mentioned

Inspiration

earlier, but it is also important that we hear what is capturing the imagination of the world. This is so that we can make our religious music more accessible to those who do not usually come to church as well as using these sounds in our own songwriting, to go beyond what the world is doing and do even better than them! This stops us from becoming stagnant and stale and keeping our feet firmly set in the past. Christian music always seems to be a decade or so behind what is current. We should be at the forefront, breaking new ground! The church should be leading the way! Search for new sounds. Try playing new chords. Experiment. Sometimes a chord that you stumble upon by accident can inspire a whole song.

How about staring from a different place in your creative process? What I mean by this is, if the lyrics or words are your natural starting point, why not try starting with a rhythm instead? Or if you usually have a melody that you are humming as a starting point, why not try starting with a general theme? Mix it up and see what happens.

Other things I do in order to stoke the fires of creativity within me is to deliberately seek out inspiring things. For example, streaming a video that has an inspiring story, watching some inspiring preaching on TV, reading an inspiring book. I also go to art galleries and scenic places. In my home I try to surround myself with inspiring things. Most of my writing is done at home and especially in the room where I tend to write, I find it helpful to have inspiring pictures and objects around me.

This reminds me of when I was writing a song a few years ago. I was playing my guitar in my bedroom and I was trying to write a warfare song. I had a verse and was struggling to find a chorus. As I was playing and meditating and just singing whatever came to mind. I glanced on my wall where my calendar was opened to the month of March. That was it. Just seeing that word had a domino effect in my mind. The chorus began to form around the concept of a marching army! You see, inspiration can come from anywhere.

As a songwriter it is highly likely that you are a very creative person. I believe it is important for us to keep practising to release our creativity in as many ways as possible. One of these ways that I discovered a while ago is painting. I am no artist! But I do enjoy experimenting with the different colours and creating new and exciting effects on the canvas. I prefer more abstract art so I just paint curious shapes and splash colours everywhere. In the end, the pictures I end up with are not that great, but that is beside the point. The object of the exercise is to release my creativity. And I do feel more creative and inspired after painting.

Inspiration

Personally, I find that stress and being excessively busy as well as a busy family life with a young family are barriers to creativity. One of the keys to success in terms of songwriting that I have discovered over the years is to be intentional. This means making a concerted effort to make the space and time needed for the creative process to happen. I know that if something isn't in my diary, it's not going to happen. So, blocking out some time on a weekly or monthly basis can be a great leap forward in developing ones songwriting skills.

Spending time with other creative people can also spark something in your creative mind. I have a few particular friends of mine whom I know stir up the creativity within me. Whenever I visit them, I know that either we will write a song together, or I will leave with a buzz, eager to release my creativity again.

I find that going to Christian conferences, songwriting workshops and worship songwriting retreats also have the desired effect. Just being around other people who are releasing their creativity can draw creativity out of you.

If you don't have the luxury of going on a retreat with others, perhaps a day away on your own from the hustle and bustle of life can give you the time and space needed to spend a focused amount of time with God as well as the intentional pursuit of songwriting.

I also find going away somewhere different on holiday also stimulates creativity. Sometimes it's just a new place or change in routine that can help me see the world in a different way. Some years ago, I was on a holiday to Jersey, one of the Channel Islands. On my second day there, I spent all morning just writing. I wrote two complete songs as well as jotting down lots of ideas and chords for other songs, that I will work on later.

A holiday is a good idea, but I certainly can't afford to take one every week. So, another way to stimulate creativity is to carve out some creative space in your weekly routine. Some lucky worship leaders I know are able to take a 'creative day'[5] once a week to relax and engage in creative things such as going for a walk, reading, resting and writing songs. If you have a full-time job you may not have the luxury of 'creative days'. I try to carve out a creative 'hour' on a Thursday. This could be to write songs but doesn't have to be exclusively focussed on songwriting. I have found simply engaging in the creative process of writing helps me when I am wanting to write a song at a later date. Why not give it a try? How about writing poetry, a handwritten letter

---

[5]Idea of 'creative days' taken from Tim Hughes and Al Gordon, Seminar given at Worship Central Retreat, May 2007. Used by permission.

Inspiration

to a friend, or a blog? Just exercise your creativity in a variety of creative ways. Get your creative cogs turning so that when you do come to write a song you are on familiar territory, using creative muscles that are strong from being in regular use.

Another freeing thing to realise is that you do not have to stick to your preferred genre of songwriting when creative expression is your goal. Songwriter and worship leader Geraldine Latty says: "Songwriters are creatives who love words! They love exploring words, defining words, playing with words and sometimes they put those words to music. So, don't feel confined to simply writing a so-called 'worship' song. We are writers, so go ahead and enjoy the creative process of writing for a range of musical expressions."[6]

I realise that we are all different, so some of the things that work for me will not work for you. Try them out by all means, but I want to encourage you to discover for yourself those things that inspire you and stimulate your creativity. Once you have discovered what these things are, don't stop trying to make space in your life to pursue them.

---

[6] Geraldine Latty, Feedback Panel at Resound Worship Songwriting Retreat, July 2019. Used by Permission.

Rearrangement[7]

There's nothing new under the sun

Just a rearrangement of words

or notes

or colours

or textures

or actions

Plucked from thin air seemingly.

But are they inspired?

If so, by whom

Or what?

The soul of man or the spirit of God?

All good things come from God

All, not a few,

or random.

---

[7] 'Rearrangement', poem written by Anna Smith, Copyright © 2006. Used by permission.

But are these good, these rearrangements?

All, or just some?

By their fruit you know them.

Is a viewer, or listener, or reader, or critic

More whole at the end

or less?

If more, then reach for the inspiration

Extend yourself to let it

Rearrange your medium

in patterns of beauty.

© *2006 Anna Smith*

CHAPTER THREE

Basic Ingredients

One of my guilty pleasures is to watch cookery shows on TV. Sometimes I enjoy the programme so much that I buy the cookery book based on the series. Quite often I don't really use the book very much but sometimes I come across a few go-to recipes that work really well for me, so I use them again and again. One thing I have noticed is that amongst the various recipe books I have, there are certain dishes or cakes that are pretty much identical to each other. I mean, how many different ways can you make a Victoria Sponge? In fact, the basic recipe is unaltered between the different books written by different authors: 200g butter, 200g sugar, 200g flour and 4 eggs. The way the chefs make it their own is to tweak or add to the basic elements. One may use raspberry jam, while another may use strawberry. How about fresh berries instead of the jam? Maybe reduce the butter content a little to make it have a few less calories? But the basic elements are the same. If you change things too much it won't work and you will end up with a mess, not a cake.

The same is true for songwriting. Songs have some basic ingredients that need to be included for your end product to be an actual song, and not a mess. Just as chefs can make some tweaks and minor adjustments, so can we. But in essence we need the basic ingredients in place for us to end up with a song.

The basic ingredients of a song are: words, structure, melody, rhythm, and harmony.

Words

The words, also called lyrics, are the part of the song that convey the direct meaning or intention of the song. Words can create images in our minds or help us to explore ideas. They are a way of expressing emotion and as such can also be the point of emotional connection with others, although I do believe that the music, or harmony, can also be emotional.

For a song to make sense it's a good idea to keep the song focussed on one central theme. A mixture of themes leaves the listener, or those joining in with the singing, confused and lost.

Try to choose words that not only have a good rhythm to them, created by the syllables (see chapter 5) but also chosen because they say exactly what you are trying to express in a clear and understandable way.

When writing lyrics it is also important to bear in mind your intended audience. When I write worship songs I try to avoid using Christian clichés as well as words that are quite far removed from the normal-person-on-the-street's experience. I want my songs to be understandable by those who are not Christians yet, or those who are new followers of Jesus. So, I avoid using language that is too deep theologically, unless of course the song unpacks and explains the complicated word or phrase. This does not mean that I avoid the more complex themes. I just try to express them with language that can be more easily understood.

Poetic devices such as rhyme can be used most effectively in songwriting and I explore this and more in Chapter 5.

Structure

All songs should have a clear structure. There are a variety of structures so select one that best suits the type of song you are trying to write. A common structure in Christian songwriting, especially for corporate worship, is: Verse 1, Chorus, Verse 2, Chorus (repeated), Bridge, Chorus (repeated), End.

More traditional hymns may just have a series of verses with a refrain that is repeated at the end of each verse, or just verses one after the other until the end is reached.

You get the idea.

The basic building blocks for creating a structure are: introduction, verses, pre-chorus, chorus, bridge, instrumental. You can have various sections repeating, or a few verses first before the first chorus comes in.

Don't feel pressured into using all the structural building blocks in the same song. Quite often, less is more! Various elements of song structure are influenced by trends and fashions, so pay attention to what other songwriters in your genre are doing. Don't feel that you have to follow the trends, but certainly be aware of them.

It may be a good idea to select a structure for your song alongside your theme. Then you can plot basic points of your song's story as you work through the structure. This may help focus your lyrical choices when you reach the different sections.

For example, the verse can introduce the theme then the chorus is a response to the theme. Verse two, which follows the chorus, needs to either explore the theme again but in a different way to the first verse, or it needs to develop and move the theme or the story of the song forward.

Melody

The melody of a song is the tune that is often sung. This tune could be played by a lead instrument as well as being sung, but the trend in more modern music is for the lead vocal to sing the melody line with the music supporting it by providing a harmony underneath.

When I write a worship song that is intended for others to join in with there are certain considerations that I try to think about. The first thing I do is to make sure that the melody of the verses stays the same from one verse to another. This is so that when someone hears the melody once, they can feel safe to join in with it the second time round and won't be met with any surprises that may cause them to opt out of singing the rest of the song. Similarly, the melody in the chorus needs to be predictable and consistently follow the same pattern if people are to sing along.

Within the verses themselves, try to repeat a line's melodic pattern again, either straight away, or alternate lines etc. There are various options available but try to avoid having a completely different melody for every single line as this makes it very difficult for someone to join in with as it is not predictable enough.

If you are writing a song for performance, then only the performer needs to know how the melody goes. You can be freer and feel less restricted in the direction the melody takes.

When writing congregational worship songs, I also try to pay attention to the range of the melody. What is the lowest and the highest note in the whole song being sung? I know there are differences between male and female vocals – we often transpose songs in my church band depending upon who is leading – but making decisions with your melody that aid congregational engagement means that your song needs to not be too low or too high. There is more on this idea in Chapter 4.

Rhythm

A song's rhythm is its heartbeat. It is what you tap your feet along with or clap your hands to. It's what helps to give a song a

Basic Ingredients

sense of joyfulness, or sadness, or stillness. The rhythm is a song's underlying rhythmic pulse and is often called the 'beat' or the 'groove'.

There are a few parts to a song's rhythm. Firstly, you have the time signature. This is how many beats there are in each bar. Usually this is 4/4 (which means four beats in a single bar). But there are other key signatures that help to give a different feel to a song such as 3/4 or 6/8.

Secondly you have the speed of the song. This is a song's tempo and can sometimes be referred to as the BPM (Beats Per Minute). You can calculate a song's BPM by counting all the beats of a song you can hear in 15 seconds. Then multiply that number by four to find how many beats there are per minute. If you are playing along to a metronome or a click-track the bleeps or clicks are set to a certain BPM in order to try to keep your playing or singing at a consistent speed that suits the song best.

Thirdly the rhythmic pattern of a song is created by stress patterns and syncopation. This is created by both the way in which the instruments are played as well as how the words are sung. Usually, the first beat of a bar is stressed more strongly than the others. However, if the bar has more than three beats in it, there is usually another stressed note in the middle of the bar:

ONE two THREE four.

Syncopation plays off the basic pattern of stressed notes that is mentioned above. It is a deliberate altering of the stress pattern which is created by stressing an offbeat (a note that is not on the beat). So basically, syncopation moves the stresses of a rhythm to a different place where one would not naturally expect to hear them.

Harmony

The harmony is basically the chords that are played in a song. These are determined by the key signature as this tells you which notes and chords will sound good together, and purposefully leaves out those that sound bad.

The key signature determines the scale of notes that can be used in a particular piece of music. It will also determine how many sharps and flats are in your chosen key. By knowing how many sharps and flats you are dealing with, as indicated by the start of a piece of sheet music, you can figure out what key that piece of music is written in. If you are not very good at reading sheet music another way of determining the key that a song is written in is to try to find the *root* note. If the end of the chorus sounds 'complete' it is more than likely landing on the root note of the

Basic Ingredients

scale. If it sounds like it still needs to be resolved, or is moving elsewhere, it is not the root note.

A particularly helpful thing to know is which chords will fit in with which key. This saves time with stumbling about trying to find chords that sound right together through trial and error. I am not an expert at music theory, so I basically use the internet to find the information. I simply type into a search engine a phrase such as 'what chords are in the key of E' and a wealth of information appears. I prefer switching my results view to 'Images' as I like the uncluttered way the information is presented. By looking at the diagrams I am told the chords of that scale. So the key of E has the following possible chords within it:

E, F#m, G#m, A, B, C#m, D#dim.

The search results also include images of which keys to play on a keyboard or which strings to press on a guitar, which are all very useful.

If you are using a guitar as your primary instrument for composing, you can change the key you are playing in without altering the chord shapes by using an ingenious invention called a capo. Capos are also useful in helping guitar players to play songs in keys that have tricky chord shapes. You simply transpose the song to a key that has easier chords to play and place the capo on the correct fret to change the tuning of the strings. Together this makes you play the right chords in the correct key without the difficulty of having to use chord shapes that are difficult to make.

If you start off writing a song and it is too high, or to low, you may want to experiment with a capo to change the key that the song is in to make it easier to sing. Then using a guitar transposing guide (again have a look on the internet – there are so many of these out there). You can then work out what key you are actually playing in.

CHAPTER FOUR

Questions to ask Yourself

Before departing on the journey of writing a song, there are certain things you should ask yourself. These questions will help to focus the song writing process and ultimately produce a song fit for the purpose for which it was written. Here are a few helpful things to consider:

What is the Theme?

The most important thing to decide when writing a song is *what!* What are you writing about? You need to decide upon a theme for the song. Now during times of inspiration, it may be difficult to fix your mind on a theme and say 'Ok, this is the theme, now let's write'. Personally, I don't worry about theme when I'm just in the zone, and worshipping. I just allow myself to sing whatever comes out. This is where the ideas and themes are birthed. It is upon re-visiting the song that a conscious decision as to the theme of the song needs to be taken. Having a theme is important as it keeps our mind, and indeed the song, focused on one point or aspect of God. Don't get too complex. There have been many times when I have written a song and have discovered that there are two themes occurring in it. There are actually two separate songs there! So I've had to dissect the song and create two new ones centred on the different themes. A theme gives a song its cohesion. It is the skeleton around which a song gets its shape, direction and character.

There have also been times when the starting point for a song has been the theme. I start out with a clear theme in mind that I want to write about. It may mean I need to do some research about it if I don't know enough. It is also useful to jot down key words and phrases as you are digging into the theme to use as a 'word bank' when writing lyrics.

Once you have a theme, the next thing you need to decide is how you are going to develop that theme throughout the song. A song is like a journey. You need to start somewhere, and ultimately arrive somewhere else. This may mean rearranging the verses or developing the climax of the song in the chorus, but still leaving a bit to be discovered in subsequent verses. The structuring of the song will help transport you from one transition of the journey to the other. Do not get stuck in one or two set structures. Experiment! Maybe you only need the chorus right at the end of the song, or maybe the chorus is only a single line refrain. Or perhaps there is no chorus at all, like so many wonderful hymns.

Where is the Destination?

As in a journey, you need to know the destination before you depart. You need to know where you are going so that when you get there you know that you have achieved your goal. So how does this fit with song writing? When writing a song, we need to determine the purpose of the song and its intended audience.

For example, we could write a song to be sung in a band setting, aimed at performance at a gig. I find writing songs like this easier as one is not bound by so many 'rules' as in congregational song writing. Here, songs can have complicated lyrical movements, strange melodies and notes. This is because only a limited number of people need to be able to sing and play the song (the band). So there is a lot of freedom to express ideas and to embark on a bit of musical experimentation. If the song works for the band and the singers who will be performing it, then that's great!

Congregational songwriting is more difficult. By this I mean there are more 'rules' around which the song has to fit. Because the intended audience is not merely listening to the music but are also expected to engage with it and sing along to it, more consideration of the congregation needs to be taken into account. Songs like this should be kept simple rhythmically, lyrically and structurally. Remember, some of the people singing the song are most probably unmusical. Also, musicians in church bands, although they have a willing heart, may not be as skilled as you would hope. If songs are too complicated, they will not be sung in a congregational setting. However, I am not suggesting you write a cheesy, cheap song. No! Keep the content fresh. Find new ways to express an old idea. Look for new ways of saying something. Search for new chords and sounds. But keep it simple. The key to congregational song writing is to keep asking yourself, 'Will my congregation be able to sing this?'.

When writing lyrics for a congregational song, a little bit of syncopation is alright, and this will add a modern flavour to it, but too much syncopation, or if it occurs in unexpected places, will confuse the congregation. Likewise, song structure should be straight forward. For example: Verse 1, Chorus, Verse 2, Chorus, Verse 3, Chorus repeated to end. You can add interest by including a Bridge that fits in between repeated Chorus sections. You could also use a Pre-Chorus that comes in just before the Chorus, although this has fallen out of fashion in recent years.

Is there Fluid Progression?

View your song as a story. There needs to be a clear beginning, middle and end. By the time your song is finished those listening to it or singing it should know that they have reached the end. Similarly, you don't want to strand them hanging from a cliff in the middle of the story either, by not resolving a build up in lyric, melody or instrumentation. Try to create a flow and a clear link between the lyrics in the verses into the chorus. Having a theme will help this. Look at your verses and decide where your story is beginning. Let us look at the song 'Ten Thousand Thousand' (on page 59 and 60) to help me explain this.

It begins addressing God directly, and this is continued throughout. It then moves to asking God to accept this song of worship.

The second verse talks about God as creator and creation responding to Him. The chorus is a reflection of creation's response, but it also includes the singer as they are now joining creation's response in worship.

The third verse moves on from the first two. The preceding verses enable verse three to let the singer now express their praise directly to God.

Can you see? Creation had to be created first, before it could respond. The story had to start at the beginning.

Ten Thousand Thousand [8]

VERSE 1

Lifter of the humble one, defender of the weak

Lover of this ransomed soul, give flight unto my speech

VERSE 2

Creator of all time and space, creation now responds

The planets and the stars cry out, to you the holy One

CHORUS

Ten thousand thousand praise Your name

And with one voice we all proclaim

The earth resounds with your great fame

You are God, You are God, You are God

---

[8] 'Ten Thousand Thousand' Copyright © 2007 Matt McChlery. Used by permission.

Songcraft

VERSE 3

Joining with creations song

The song of the redeemed

I raise my heart, I lift my voice

To You the holy One, holy One

BRIDGE

For no one and nothing, is greater than You,

Is greater than You

© *2007 Matt McChlery*

Questions to Ask Yourself

What is the Shape of the Melody? [9]

Hopefully your melody will contain differences between the different sections – verses will sound different to the chorus, for example.

Does the shape of the melody fit with the words of the song? Have you got words such as 'bow down' or 'bend low' where it would be good to have the melody descending at those moments, or words like 'lift up' or 'rose again' where an ascending melody would add weight, meaning and importance to what is being sung?

Try to make sure important words are stressed. Usually this happens on beats 1 and 3 in a song written in 4/4. What is the highest note in the song? Does a key word fall on that note? If not, why not?

To what extent does your melody move? Does it move in small steps – from one note to a neighbouring note? Or does it skip, jumping from one note to another that is a few notes higher or lower than it? Or does it stay on the same note for a while? It may be worth changing how your melody moves from one section to another. For example, your verse might move in small steps, then when you reach the chorus it makes bigger jumps.

---

[9] Adapted from a workshop and handout by Matt Osgood at the Resound Worship Songwriting Retreat, July 2019. Used by permission.

Songcraft

The second verse mirrors the first, moving in the same way, as does the chorus. To add colour to the bridge you may decide to keep everything on the same note, or two notes. Then back to the chorus with its big leaps.

Are there any distinctive leaps (or hooks) in your melody? If not, could there be?

How much does your melody centre around the strong or stable notes of the scale you are using? These strong notes are often the first and fifth notes of the scale as opposed to the weaker or less stable notes which are the second, fourth, seventh or sixth notes.

A good example of this is a song called 'What a Beautiful Name' written by Brooke Ligertwood and Ben Fielding, recorded by Hillsong Worship. Look it up online and listen to it. If you can get hold of the sheet music, or a lead sheet that just notates the melody line, it will help you to see what I am talking about visually.

The song starts with verse one. The first line sits on the same note for a bit, then descends in steps from one neighbouring note to the next. Into the second line we get a five note jump up to start the second line. Next the melody jumps up a space of two notes to hit the next word, which is the highest note in the verse, and notice it lands on an important word 'God'. From this point the melody descends in even steps moving one note down each step, with a one syllable word sitting neatly on each note. This pattern is then repeated to complete the verse.

We have now arrived at the chorus. Notice how the first seven notes are the same. It is okay to repeat a note in succession if there are other interesting things happening at the same time, such as interesting lyrics or the harmony of the chords are shifting underneath the melody line. In this song it is the richness of the lyric which carries the song at this point. After the first seven notes, the melody steps down one note and now this note is repeated ten times before moving down one more step to complete the first phrase of the chorus. The next phrase begins with a jump up to the note the chorus originally started in and then descends in sequential steps down.

The second part of the chorus mirrors the first with lyric and melody (the same note repeated seven times). But now it moves into a section that moves about melodically, jumping up, then down and then up again. This adds interest to the melody, providing a contrast to sticking on the same note which happens quite a lot, as well as emphasising the lyrics in this section.

The chorus ends with another repetition of the melody that started the chorus.

We then have verse two which behaves in exactly the same way as verse one. Keeping the melody nice and predictable for those who want to join in and sing along.

After another chorus the song launches into the bridge. A distinction is made here melodically as the melody jumps a lot. Not a single note is repeated immediately after itself like in other sections. The gaps between the jumps vary between one and two notes and move up and down like a wave.

The bridge builds up in intensity and then when the chorus comes back in with the same seven notes in succession, it really lands the melody. It brings it back down to earth thus emphasising the weight of the words being sung in the chorus as well as resolving the intensity that had been created in the bridge.

Are you Hitting the High Notes?

Have you noticed how some worship songs are just pitched too high? This happens especially on recordings and I often find myself transposing worship songs into a lower key to enable my congregation to sing it more comfortably. Now I've been told that using a higher key is best for massive worship gatherings or when recording, however this often doesn't translate into accessible congregationally friendly keys.

Questions to Ask Yourself

If you are wanting to create impact with an octave jump, which is fairly common, the verses are often pretty low to enable the jump later into the chorus. But remember, a lot of the congregation will not be able to join in with an octave jump and will probably sing the whole song at an uncomfortable pitch that is either too high or too low for their range.

Male and female ranges differ too. We have our worship songs at church printed out in two keys, one for when a male is singing lead vocals and the other for when a female leads. This is one reason why when I lead at larger gatherings or conferences, I try to get a mixture of 'voices' taking the lead – sometimes male, the other female – so that at some point through the event everyone gets to sing at a pitch that is comfortable for them and therefore enabling their engagement and enhancing their worship.

If you are writing a congregational song try to keep your melody sitting between a low Bb (Bb2 - in pitch notation) up to top D (D5 – in pitch notation) as this is the range most people find comfortable or at least manageable.

Are there any Dynamics?

As you tell the story of your song, you need to use expression. A monotone reading of a story is very boring and uninteresting.

Similarly, a song needs to have expression injected into it through the way it is sung as well as the way it is played.

Dynamics can be created in a variety of ways. You should always aim to have an ebb and flow, and increase and then decrease in volume, like waves. Linear dynamic[10] is where the whole band increases or decreases the volume of the music together. Terraced dynamic can be created by various instruments or voices either adding to the sound or dropping out of the sound where required. You can also use a motif, or instrumental hook, to help add colour and interest to the song.

A theme provides a skeleton to work around, structure makes sure all the bones go in the right place, lyrics put flesh on the skeleton and dynamics add the details or features.

Dynamics are important to the life and development of a song; but they need to be used with sensitivity. Make sure that the dynamics chosen fit the song's emotion and mood.

Is it a Mouthful?

Another important question to ask yourself, especially if you intend your song to be sung by others, is 'Do the words roll off the tongue?' As you sing the song, check to make sure that the

---

[10] Idea of 'linear and terraced dynamics' taken from Tim Hughes, Passion For Your Name, Kingsway Publications 2003, p.89. Used by permission.

words you have chosen are easy to sing. Sometimes certain words or combinations of words are particularly difficult to sing as they 'stick' in your mouth. They do not flow smoothly and easily from one to the other. If you have a mouthful of words, spit them out and write some new ones!

Is it Theologically Accurate?

If you are writing songs to be sung in church, it is of vital importance that they are theologically accurate. In other words, what the song says needs to express the truth of God's Word. As songwriters we have the increasing responsibility to make sure our songs are theologically sound as people are more likely to remember the songs they have sung in church rather than the sermon. What an exciting time to be living in as a songwriter. What a responsibility to carry. Songs are forming people's belief systems more and more so it is important that they contain substance and truth.

A good way to do this is to talk to your pastor at church about what you do as a songwriter and ask them if they wouldn't mind giving you some theological feedback. I often email songs that I think are near completion to my pastor to receive his feedback. Often everything is fine but there have been some occasions where there has been some theological point I had missed or had not expressed completely.

For example if you are writing a song that mentions God the Father and God the Son, but does not mention God the Holy Spirit, the wholeness of the trinity is being neglected. It is important to sing about all aspects of the trinity in this instance.

Another thing to think about is 'what is missing?' What is missing in the theological diet of the songs sung at your church?[11]. I encourage you to review the songs you have sung at church over the last few months and try to identify if there are any theological gaps. Then go about trying to redress the imbalance. As songwriters, we should also try to identify gaps within the repertoire of our church's songs. What theological themes are missing? Which aspects of God's character do we not have any songs about? What parts of God's Word are we not singing? As well as nourishing the theological health of the songs you sing at church, exploring new themes can also lead to spur on your creativity.

Does it Help Me to Worship?

Finally, and most importantly for the congregational songwriter, you need to check to see if your song helps you to worship. Matt Redman puts it like this: "The best congregational melodies

---

[11] Idea of 'gaps in our theology' taken from Rev. Graham Cray, Seminar given at Passion For Your Name, August 2006. Used by permission.

Questions to Ask Yourself

work *in* worship because they begin *as* worship"[12]. This comes back to the destination of your song. If you intend your song to be used within a worship setting, you need to be able to worship with it on your own first, and then with the church. It is a real blessing when 'home grown' songs are sung within the church as they can bring a blessing that far outweighs more widespread songs. This is because the songwriter is tuned in to the life and experiences of the church and the songs they write can reflect the journey of that particular church.

---

[12] Matt Redman, The Heart Of Worship Files, Kingsway Publications 2003, p.31. Used by permission.

CHAPTER FIVE

Practical Tips

If golden nuggets of songwriting advice is what you are after, you will find some in this chapter.

Re-visit and Re-work

Songwriting is a bit like gold mining in that it is a process of refinement. You need to dig deep in order to find the precious ore that is buried within a whole lot of rubbish. Then once you have found the gold, it needs to be smelted down and refined, burning away all the impurities until all that remains is pure gold.

I want to encourage you to write everything you get, every phrase, every weird idea, or thought that captures your attention.

Don't be afraid to write rubbish songs. As I mentioned earlier, an old idea or phrase may be just what you need at a later date to finish a different song. Don't dismiss the frustrating times when you feel you've not succeeded, rather embrace them and learn from them. Digging down to find the ore, there is a lot of worthless soil along the way. You've got to dig it out of you, or write it out of you, in order to get it out of the way. Once you've done a lot of digging and rubbish removal, you will soon find the gold vein in the mountain.

Once you've found your nugget of a song, don't think you have finished the process. Come back to it, re-work the ideas, ask yourself some of the questions mentioned in the previous chapter, run the song past other experienced song writers for feedback. This is all part of the refinement process which helps to distil a song and knock any rough edges off it before you arrive at the finished article: "My heart bursts its banks, spilling beauty and goodness. I pour it out in a poem to the king, shaping the river into words." (The Message, Psalm 45:1)

Co-writing

Writing songs with other people can be a refreshing experience, or a terribly frustrating one. I've found that the better I know the person or people I am co-writing with, the easier the process is. It's amazing how God likes to birth things out of relationship. So, cultivate and invest in the relationships you have with your fellow musicians and song writer friends.

I have found that when arranging a co-writing session, I have to be very deliberate about it. Sometimes this may mean planning months in advance and committing to the date and writing it down in my diary, then buying the train tickets. It's amazing how busy life can get and how our time can be totally swallowed up. Be deliberate and proactive.

It also helps a lot to arrive at a co-writing session with something already prepared. Having part of a melody, or a cool riff you've been working on, or even a verse and half a chorus can help a lot. This helps to provide a focus for your time together and a stimulus from where other things may spring. Be open-minded. Listen to other points of view and be willing to change things or make compromises. Feel free to experiment. Remember if it goes horribly wrong don't worry. You can come back to that song at a later date and try again.

Mnemonic Value

Mnemonic value refers to a pattern of words or music that is easily remembered. It is vitally important that the songs we write are memorable and recognisable. There are subtle ways that this can be achieved within a song. A song that has a strong repeated motif or a distinctive bass line helps the listener to identify the song simply by hearing a few notes and helps them to remember it.

Countermelodies can also provide a strong mnemonic hook in a song. This is where a certain instrument plays a melody line that is different from the sung melody, often in the introduction and sometimes this countermelody is repeated just before the chorus or in an instrumental section.

Words also have the ability to be strongly mnemonic. A carefully crafted phrase or chorus line has the potential to capture someone's imagination. Great words combined with a catchy melody are a sure winner. If you can't get a song out of your head, its mnemonics have worked. Try to write songs that people will still be singing days later while they are doing the washing up.

Poetic Devices

There are some tricks used by poets that work well in songs too that help aid the mnemonic value of a song, or more simply help the song hang together well.

Metaphor can be used within a song to help add freshness to the way something is described. It enables song writers to explore old ideas in new ways. However, metaphor can be very obscure at times so you need to make absolutely sure that you've made it clear elsewhere in the song what it is you are actually talking about. If it is too obscure and creates more confusion than clarity, don't use it.

Simile is similar to metaphor. This allows you to compare the features or characteristics of one thing with another. This means that you are making it clear what it is you are talking about and is therefore less ambiguous. Many Christian songwriters have used similes in their songs and have achieved some fantastic results that have breathed new life into tired themes. However, you must beware of the cheesy Christian cliché here. All too often perfectly good songs are ruined by the use, or overuse, of common clichés. Use the cliché as a starting point, and then re-work that idea. Think of other things that can be compared with the thing you are describing. Things that are less obvious or things that have not necessarily been used to describe that object in quite that way before, but achieves a dramatic and effective result.

Assonance is when sounds within words rhyme with the same sound in other words. It could be vowel sounds that rhyme (e.g. s_o_nnet, p_o_rridge), or the use of an identical consonant (e.g. _t_all, _t_imid, _T_ony). Alliteration is the occurrence of the same letter or sound in words that are nearby. Assonance and alliteration help to give cohesion to a verse or chorus and helps it hang together well. If you do use these devices be aware that too much can be distracting. It works best when their presence goes unnoticed. It becomes a problem when they start distracting people from the message of the song, or even worse, from engaging with God. You could also run into the trap of making that group of words difficult to sing. Try to avoid using a series of hard consonants such as k, s, and t, as they are harder to sing in quick succession.

Rhyme is another extremely useful poetic device for the song writer. However, sometimes I feel that certain song writers fall into the trap of trying to make absolutely everything they write rhyme. There is no rule saying that all songs ever written need to have rhyme in them. No, some of the best songs I've heard have absolutely no rhyme in them at all. If you are caught in the trap of having to write rhyming songs, I challenge you to try to deliberately write a song with no rhyme. You may be surprised by the results. Having said this, rhyme can be a useful tool if not used in excess. Songs with too much rhyme often sound over the top or childish. When I use rhyme in my songs I try to let the rhymes occur naturally as I'm singing my ideas. Often I find that it is only alternate line endings that rhyme with each other. Remember, if you do decide to use a rhyming pattern, that pattern needs to be consistent throughout the song.

Practical Tips

As you sing or hum a possible melody, you are also creating a rhythm pattern for the song. The way the lyrics fit around the beat is a very important aspect of song writing. Your rhythm needs to be consistent and steady, as it sets the pace, or heartbeat for the rest of the song. Once you have your beat, you then need to try to fit your words within its parameters. A good way of doing this is by counting syllables. A syllable is the natural beat or rhythm that words make as they are spoken or sung. For example, the word 'p<u>a</u>ssi<u>o</u>n' has two syllables and the word 'w<u>o</u>rsh<u>i</u>pp<u>e</u>r' has three, whereas the word 'G<u>o</u>d' only has one. Notice how the syllable always falls on the vowel (often chord changes fall on the vowel of a word because that is where the natural rhythm of the word is found). When you are reworking a song, check to see that the same syllable pattern is being used throughout. If the first verse has five syllables in the first line, then seven syllables in the second, this pattern needs to be the same in all the other verses too. This helps to give structure to the song as well as making it a little bit more predictable for those singing it.

Songwriting Exercises

These exercises are not really intended to help you write a decent song as an outcome. The aim of them is to simply help you engage with the creative process, to use the 'muscles' needed in order to write good songs. Basically it is like going to a songwriting gym for a workout. A 100-metre sprinter isn't going to run a 100-metre race in the gym, but he is going to prepare his body in order to do it well when he does. So, treat these exercises like a workout, getting you ready and fit for when you do sit down to write a song.

Word Association – I have picked up a great exercise for songwriters from a seminar given by David Hadden[13]. All you need is a piece of paper and a pencil. Now give yourself a topic. It can be anything you like, no matter how obscure. You now have 60 seconds to write down as much as you can about your topic. It doesn't matter if all the words are joined together or if it's untidy, just write down everything you can think of. When the minute is up, count all the words you have written down about the topic. If you are doing this with another person, the one with the highest number wins! Or you could set it as a personal target to beat next time. Now think of another topic and repeat the process.

Let's use 'car' as our example. Here are my results when I first tried this exercise: *Car, fast, ignition, break, clutch, power, speed, agility, colour, stigma, status symbol, fast, formula one, Ferrari, garage,*

---

[13] 'Song writing exercise' taken from David Hadden, Seminar given at a song writer's workshop, d-B Studios, Lincoln, 2006. Used by permission.

Practical Tips

petrol, Austin Martin, tyre, pedals, steering wheel, indicator, seats, doors, windscreen wiper, hooter (horn), boot, carpets, body, seat cover, fluffy dice. (37 words was my score!).

It is actually quite challenging to do, but it gets your brain working. The more you practise brainstorming ideas like this, the easier you will find the lyrical crafting process of song writing.

Haiku Poem - Haiku poetry is an ancient Japanese artform. It must contain seventeen syllables in total: three lines of five, seven, then five. This exercise will help you focus on the syllabic content of words as well as to restrict yourself to certain syllable counts for different lines of your songs.

Learning to write songs (5 syllables)
Can be difficult and hard (7 syllables)
But is rewarding (5 syllables)

Listen and Learn – Get hold of a song you love. It doesn't matter the genre. Now sit down and listen to it. I mean *really* listen. Grab a piece of paper and jot down things you notice. What is the hook? Where does it occur? How often does it occur? Which instrument plays it? How is it structured? Is there ebb and flow? Do the dynamics rely upon the instruments getting louder, or are more instruments added as the song goes along? What is the key signature? What is the BPM? Are there any images evoked by the lyrics? How is this done? You get the idea.

First and Last – Select a topic (it can be anything) and write town the first word that fits within your topic that comes to mind. Now think of another word that starts with the same letter that the first word finished with. How many words can you think of?

This can also be used well within a group, each member taking it in turn to think of the next word. If someone gets it wrong or takes too long, they are 'out'. You can keep going until one person emerges victorious.

Here is a short example using the topic 'celebrities':

*Nelson Mandela – **A**manda Holde**n** – **N**icholas Cag**e** – **E**ddie the Eag**l**e – **E**mily Blun**t** – **T**ina Turne**r** – **R**upert Everett*

Predictive Text Challenge – type a topic into your phone. Press the space bar. Now press the middle button on predictive text five times. You should end up with six words. Use those words in a song.

Practical Tips

Syllable Gallop – The idea is to write a list of words that progressively increase in syllables based on a topic or theme. How far can you get? Try to beat your high score.

Here's a short one I have done using the theme 'musical instruments':

Drum (1) – guitar (2) – piano (3) – ukulele (4) – MIDI controller (5).

Alliteration Agility – Start by listing numbers, colours, days of the week or months of the year, or anything really, down the side of the page. Now take each word in turn and use them as a starting point to write a sentence that uses alliteration in almost every word. Here is an example of one line:

One wiggly warthog was waggling its wonderful tail.

Sensible Senses[14] – A good way to get your creative juices flowing as well as developing your ability to write interesting descriptions in your songs is to use your senses. Pick an object and describe it using the sense of smell, touch, sight, hearing and even taste. This will hopefully help your descriptions in your songwriting to become more multidimensional. Often when things are approached from different angles, new horizons emerge.

---

[14] This idea supplied by Kat Mills over a Facebook Messenger conversation on Friday 27th September 2019. Used by permission.

Prepare for Criticism

Playing your song to someone for the first time can be a nerve-racking experience. This baby you have been nurturing and growing for a while is now being exposed and opened up to scrutiny and criticism. But this is a vital part of the creative process.

I would encourage you to find a few friends who are honest and straight with you. They don't necessarily have to be songwriters themselves, although this does help, but they do need to know about music and what makes a good song. It is very unhelpful if the only responses you get are vague positives. Sometimes you play a song to someone knowing its not very good and all they say is 'That was lovely'. So, find people who are brave and can give structural criticism. They need to be able to give advice, but do it with grace and humility, in such a way as not to crush you. In return, you could also listen to some of their songs and give advice where you can. Remember, don't always pick out the negatives of a song, highlight the positives too.

Before you play your song to someone else, I suggest you prepare yourself to be open and ready to accept their feedback. Be prepared to listen and to learn and to be flexible enough to make changes. You also need to be hard as nails and determine before hand that you will not take offence by anything said.

Practical Tips

Sometimes what is suggested is rubbish, and you need to be prepared to decide for yourself whether you take the advice or not. Be discerning. Pray about your songs and ask God if it is pleasing to Him. After all, He is the one we are ultimately writing the songs for.

CHAPTER SIX

Cultural Relevance

In a world where globalisation is ever increasing and individuality seems to be decreasing, I believe it is extremely important that the songs we write capture and reflect the culture in which we live. God is a creative God and He loves diversity. Just look around you and see all the different colours and shapes and listen to all the different sounds. In His creative wisdom God made people to be different and it is within the unity of the church where we can best celebrate our differences.

Songcraft

By making our songs culturally relevant, we are further enhancing the ability that they have to engage the worshipper. To meet them through something that is familiar that then takes them closer to God. As Christians we are called to be in the world but not of the world (John 17:16-18). However, this is not to say that we cannot engage the culture around us and redeem it. We are called to be agents of change, to be the point of difference. As long as the elements we are adapting and adopting from the culture around us are biblical, we should do all we can to make them part of our 'kingdom culture'.

I want to encourage you to listen to the sounds of the culture around you. Is there a particular musical style or distinctive sound that is unique to it? There may even be indigenous instruments that help create this distinctive sound. God is the source of creation and all creativity and Satan has come along and twisted that creation. It is the church's job to go about reclaiming and redeeming those things that have been lost. In our case sounds, melodies and whole genres of music.

For a long time 'rock 'n roll' has been viewed as 'the devil's music', and indeed many of the themes and philosophies being proposed in the songs were, and still are, sinful. However, in the last decade or so, Christians have begun redeeming this genre of music. Using the sounds but changing the motivation and purpose of the songs and in the process, they have turned something selfish and sinful into something that glorifies and praises God. It's more about the position and attitude of the heart, rather than the particular sound itself.

I say this because I know in certain cultures various indigenous instruments are used in the worship of idols or false religions. In Zimbabwe, where I was born, the *mbira*, or steel piano, is one such instrument. Some may have questions whether such an instrument could be used in the worship of God, that it may be 'tainted' by sin in some way. But aren't we forgetting that we too are tainted by sin, and that we enter into worship only through God's grace? And besides, people are the ones that do the sinning, not the instruments! Let's redeem those sounds and instruments. Let's turn them back to the original purpose that God intended for them: the worship of His name.

Celebration Church, Zimbabwe

I have found no better example of cultural relevance within songwriting than the songs coming out of Celebration Church in Harare, Zimbabwe. I was part of the worship team there for a year whilst finishing my post-graduate diploma in 2002. It amazed me how seamlessly different languages were integrated within the same song and how songs could still have that distinctive African flavour and yet remain fresh and modern.

Songcraft

Don't get me wrong, not every song had an African style or a mixture of languages. There were a few that did and that was enough. It's all about finding the right balance.

Let us look at how they have achieved cultural relevance in a song called 'Toimba Ishe' by Andrew Baird and Prince Mafukidze. They have taken two languages, English and Shona, and have mixed them together very skilfully into a song. Notice how the meaning of the song holds together and is consistent all the way through. This is ideal for a multilingual society, such as Zimbabwe, but they have also remembered those who do not speak Shona and have provided the English translation of what is being sung in brackets. This aids understanding which in turn aids the worship.

The culture of Zimbabwe is also carried instrumentally in this song. It has a strong rhythm and a busy bass line, with a high pitched electric guitar being plucked above it along with a synthesiser holding everything together.

Other ways in which Celebration Church have made their songs culturally relevant is by using the bass members of the choir to subtly sing a repeated phrase or chant in Shona that sits right in the background of the sound, while the rest of the song is being sung in English over the top. This bass chanting is a common tribal African motif and is used to great effect here.

Cultural Relevance

I have also recently come across songs sung in Spanish, which have either translated and existing song into Spanish or originated in the Spanish language itself. However, they still sound very western. Wouldn't it be nice to add some indigenous Spanish or Mexican instrumentation in the musical soundscape somewhere?

Cultural relevance within a song can be achieved in a variety of ways, and the suggestions in this chapter are by no means exhaustive. Have fun experimenting!

Toima Ishe[15]

VERSE

You are my glorious King

The One in whom I trust

You are the Ancient of Days

Forever You will reign

CHORUS

Tomurumbidza (We praise)

Hallelujah, hallelujah

Tomunamata (We worship)

Hallelujah, hallelujah

Tosimudzira (We stand)

---

[15] 'Toimba Ishe' by Andrew Baird and Prince Mafukidze, Copyright © 2006 Hear The Music. Taken from the songbook 'Change The World', p.49. Used by Permission. www.celebrationmin.org

Hallelujah, hallelujah

Topururudza (We shout)

Hallelujah, hallelujah

Toimba Ishe (We sing)

You are the greatest

Toimba Ishe (We sing)

My Rock of Ages

BRIDGE

Hallelujah hosanna

Hallelujah hosanna

© *2006 Andrew Baird & Prince Mafukidze*

CHAPTER SEVEN

Sharing Your Song

The first question to ask yourself is: should I share this song?

Some songs are not for sharing but exist as personal expressions between you and God. Other songs may be for specific people and them only, for example if you were to write a song for your loved one to celebrate your anniversary. Some songs may be specifically for your local church context for a particular season.

This is not to say that songs like this should not be shared more widely. It is just sensible to consider the question.

Having said this, I have come across songs written for specific people and circumstances that have a much wider reach than originally intended. Often, personal songs have many cross-over points and people find they can relate to them easily.

If you believe that the song you have written should be shared more widely, here are a few things you should know.

Copyright

I do not claim to be a copyright expert. I do not have a law degree and I would strongly encourage you to investigate what the copyright laws are in your country, as they differ from nation to nation.

In the UK you own the copyright automatically. As soon as you write or record your idea, it belongs to you. In the past some people would post recordings and lyrics to themselves and then leave the package sealed when they received it in order to prove that on the date of postage they were in ownership of the lyrics or melodies contained within the package.

However, these days with digital technology, whenever a file is created it is date stamped which makes it much easier to prove who had the idea first by examining digital records.

Sharing Your Song

So, in the UK, as soon as you write down your song lyrics you can put © 2020 (followed by your name) at the bottom, as it is automatically copyrighted to you.

This leads to other difficulties. How can churches display the words of your songs, or broadcast them via a live stream or podcast, or print them on an order of service sheet without breeching copyright law?

This is where CCLI (Church Copyright Licensing International) comes in. CCLI is an international organisation that helps churches to overcome the problems mentioned in the previous paragraph. A church pays an annual subscription to CCLI and in return has permission to display, print, copy, broadcast the songs held on the CCLI catalogue legally. They then calculate how often a song is used and work out how much money they should pass on to the artist in royalties.

Joining CCLI can be a little difficult as you need to have a song that is currently being sung in a variety of churches for them to consider adding you to the database. It may be a little difficult, but I would still encourage you to make contact and to be persistent. It is well worth the effort. Visit ccli.com for more information.

If holding on to the copyright is not for you and you just want to let your song be used legally for free (and you not to earn anything from it) you may want to consider using the Creative Commons License. However, it is important to note that once you have released a song under Creative Commons it cannot be revoked or reversed. When you make it copyright free, it stays copyright free. So if a record label is interested, they won't be able to take that song on as the copyright for it has already been revoked, and they will very quickly lose interest.

If this is for you, look further into Creative Commons at creativecommmons.org as there are a variety of licenses to choose from that have varying levels of copyright control for your creative works.

Personally, I have retained the copyright to my songs and have my songs registered with CCLI. I also use the services of Song Solutions who administrate the catalogues of publishers and copyright holders as well as provide a worldwide service. This gives me one point of contact for all my copyright needs. They deal with a wide variety of royalty and licensing agencies around the world such as PRS, ASCAP, PPL and CCLI to name a few. This increases the reach of your songs and enables them to be used in more places in a wider variety of ways. To find out more details about the services they offer as well as who they already work with please visit songsolutions.org for more information.

Use your Platform

The first and most obvious place to share your song is amongst your friends and networks that you have already established. This may be by posting something on social media and sharing it with your friends, or if you have a website you can put a demo recording of your song on there with a chord chart and share it that way.

If you are involved with the worship band at church, it would be a good idea to have a meeting with the leader of the team and to share your song with them first. Then look to see if there was any possibility that they may be willing to sing it at church. Or maybe you can sing it for the people in your home group?

Recording

Once a song is finished and I want to let my band or a producer know what it sounds like, I use my computer and some free recording software called Audacity to record a basic version of the song. There are other audio recording software packages out there that come with all sorts of add-ons such as amplifier modelers, drum loops, virtual instruments etc. But I find Audacity is able to record multiple tracks and has some effects built in which is all I need to make a half decent recording to help share my song. I wouldn't sell the end result as my skillset is not in production so I pay the professionals to do this for me. They are the ones who use the super-expensive software and fancy features.

In order to plug my microphone and guitar into the computer I have bought a little box made by a company called Focusrite which allows me to plug my mics and instruments in one end and then connects to the computer with a USB.

I use these rough recordings in different ways. It serves as a record to remind me how the song goes as well as having something to share with my band so they can hear how it goes, catch the groove and melody etc, so that when we rehearse they already have some ideas as to how the song goes.

Most of the songs on my website are rough demos as it can be expensive to record professionally. I have found this has not stopped people from using my songs. In fact, some of the most sung songs I have written have not been recorded professionally, but have been heard on my website and local church musicians have taken it from there.

But recording songs professionally is good fun and it is great to have a top-quality product to share and point people towards.

So, if you do have the money (or if you do a bit of crowd funding) it is worth recording some of your most popular or strong songs professionally.

If you are not a singer or a musician, don't worry. There are ways and means. Have a look at the 'Useful Websites' chapter for further help and advice about recording professionally. There are some who will provide all the musicians and singers for you if that's what you need.

Distribution

By sharing your songs, and your recordings with your platform you have already started to distribute or spread your music.

Having a social media presence as well as a website is an important part of building credibility as a songwriter these days as well as widening your sphere of influence. It also shows that you are taking your music and songwriting seriously if you have invested in a website and had a few proper publicity photos taken.

Creating press releases and sending these to local and national press outlets when you release an album or EP can help raise your profile. You should also have an Electronic Press Kit (EPK) ready which contains a short biography about yourself, a description of your music and style. You may mention who influences you in there too. It should also list your social media links as well as contact details. Links to your music as well as and videos you may have online are also good to include.

EPKs are used to send your music to radio stations as well as to potential events. They are usually a PDF document (so it can be printed out if needed) but sent electronically via email so that the links can be clicked on etc.

There are various ways you can get your music onto digital sales and streaming platforms such as CD Baby and Tune Core. Again, have a look at the 'Useful Websites' chapter for more details about this.

Get Rich Quick?

Hopefully you are embarking on your songwriting journey because it is something that God has called you to do. It is often a long and lonely road that can be very difficult. It is most certainly not a road towards getting rich. Making and recording music costs a lot of money, yet people are very used to getting things for free – so selling your music is very difficult. Digital streaming sites are notorious for paying fractions of a penny for a stream, so you would need several hundred thousand streams before you actually started to see anything near a decent amount of money in your bank account. Even then, it is not a reliable source of income as people who were listening to your song last month probably aren't listening to it this month. So please don't rely on your songwriting or music making to pay the rent – it won't. But don't let this stop you. Be faithful to the call God has placed within you, use and nurture the gifts and abilities He has given you and pursue it.

CHAPTER EIGHT

The Power of Words

Music, the universal language, has long been identified as containing a power somewhere between its harmonics. Somehow, we all understand that when we are talking about 'music', we are talking about 'power'. Advertisers understand music's power of persuasion; film makers know its power of emotion. Some genres of music influence lifestyle and culture, others influence and promote self-interest, popularity and worldly lust. More godly music can sweep us into praise, bringing us to our knees in worship, or turn a heart to repentance and salvation. We can find strength and encouragement well up within us as we listen to certain songs – there is power in music!

This we know, but do we have any idea how much power a song, or music in general, actually wields? There are far-reaching spiritual dimensions to music and song that we don't know about. Here is an example from my own life where a fraction of the power of a song was revealed to me. I grasped and understood this much, but I know it is only the tip of the iceberg. "We don't yet see things clearly. We're squinting in a fog, peering through a mist. But it won't be long before the weather clears and the sun shines bright! We'll see it all then, see it all as clearly as God sees us, knowing him directly just as he knows us!" (1 Corinthians 13:12, The Message)

Youth Encounter, Zimbabwe

I was leading worship at a 'Youth Encounter'; a youth camp in Zimbabwe. It was nearly the final night and the preacher was praying for people. Some were being filled with the Spirit, some were watching, and a few demons were beginning to manifest in a couple of others. There was one girl in particular whose demonic deliverance was taking an extremely long time. People had been praying for her for about an hour when I joined them. I stayed and prayed for a while, but this demon would not

The Power of Words

budge. The girl was mumbling things in Shona (an indigenous African language) so we quickly called someone to interpret. The demon was communicating. It was laughing at us because we were too 'young' and it was boasting how much stronger it was than us. Its pride and arrogance made me feel ill, however, we were not ones to give up, so we soldiered on and kept praying.

During this time we learned from the girl's sister that this girl's grandmother whom she had stayed with for a very long time was a *nanga* (witchdoctor) who are heavily involved in occultism. So, we knew we had a tough job ahead of us. No matter what we said or prayed, nothing would happen.

Then all of a sudden, I felt a stirring within me saying 'sing'. So gently and quietly I began to sing over this girl '*Hakuna wakaita sa Jesu*' which means 'There's no one, there's no one like Jesus' (The demon did not respond to English, so a Shona song was needed). As the song was released and sung, the Holy Spirit began to move. Jesus showed up! A dramatic change came over the girl. The demon started loosing its grip and within minutes, it was gone.

The power of the song to usher in the presence of God, and the name of Jesus, set that girl free! The Bible tells us that it is with music that we can shatter high places in the spirit realm and change nations: "You shall have a song as in the night when a holy festival is kept, and gladness of heart as when one goes with a flute, to come into the mountain of the Lord, to the Mighty One of Israel. The Lord will cause His glorious voice to be heard, and show the descent of His arm, with the indignation of His anger and the flame of a devouring fire, with scattering, tempests, and hailstones. For through the voice of the Lord Assyria will be beaten down, as He strikes with the rod. And in every place where the staff of punishment passes, which the Lord lays on him, it will be with tambourines and harps; and in battles of brandishing He will fight with it" (Isaiah 30:29-32, NKJV).

A Wholesome Tongue

"A wholesome tongue is a tree of life, but perverseness in it breaks the spirit" (Proverbs 15:4, NKJV). As songwriters we have an awesome responsibility. As the first chapter of Genesis shows, words have a creative power. We can use them to build up and to destroy. The power of our words has a spiritual base and we should be wise not to forget this. Be careful with your words. We have been given delegated responsibility to speak and sing into the lives and spirits of the congregations who sing our songs. We need to safeguard our lives and be careful not to let perverseness enter our spirits. "For out of the overflow of the heart the mouth speaks" (Matthew 12:34, NIV). If we are not safeguarding our hearts, the words we write and sing will be affected and our ministries could become fruitless and destructive. Strive to live a godly life so that your tongue will be wholesome. Establish the tree of life in your life then the rivers of true living water will be able to flow out from within you.

"With the tongue we praise our Lord and Father, and with it we curse men, who have been made in God's likeness. Out of the same mouth come praise and cursing. My brothers, this should not be. Can both fresh water and salt water flow from the same spring? My brothers, can a fig tree bear olives, or a grape vine bear figs? Neither can a salt spring produce fresh water" (James 3:9-12, NIV).

Fruit That Lasts

A good friend of mine once challenged me to live an extraordinary life for God. We should all be aware that we are continually producing fruit in our lives, good or bad. This fruit then leads on to the sowing of seeds. Just like in the physical realm, our fruit is determined by the kind of person we are deep inside. The root determined the fruit. As in the physical or natural realm, fruit usually only lasts for a season, then it is gone. As each new season comes, so the trees strive to produce a new harvest. This is not a bad thing in itself. We too must continue to try to produce new fruit which should be birthed out of our alive and growing relationship with Jesus. Although we may have produced fruit yesterday or last year, we need to be seeking fresh revelation, a new understanding of God. We need to be eating the fresh manna of today as yesterday's manna is no longer able to sustain us. So new fruit is good and necessary.

However, my friend led me to this passage: "You did not choose me, but I chose you and appointed you to go and bear fruit – fruit that will last" (John 15:16, NIV). This inspired and challenged me deeply. Although producing fruit is good, God has a higher calling and purpose for us. His vision for our lives is something far beyond what we could hope, dream or imagine. God is a big God, and he thinks on his own scale – a large one! God doesn't just want us to produce fruit, but fruit that lasts. Fruit that has no 'use by' label stuck on it. Fruit that will continue to give nourishment and life to the body of Christ for endless generations. A fruit that will stand the test of time. What an awesome call and what an amazing responsibility!

How can we do this? The answer is simple really – we can't. But God can; through us! If we try to birth lasting fruit in the flesh, it will not last. Flesh and the physical realm by its very nature are not eternal. It will all pass away. Lasting fruit needs to be born of the spirit. It needs to be grown in the kingdom and planted there, with His people. God wants us to make our lives count during our time on earth. We need to be looking to see how we can leave our mark on history.

Some good examples of lasting fruit are some of the ancient hymns, and some more recent choruses that you know, have and will stand the test of time. God's truth and anointing are resting just as heavily upon them today as when they were first written. Some hymns that fit into this category, in my point of view, are 'Crown Him with Many Crowns', 'Be Thou my Vision', 'Hark the Herald Angels Sing' and 'Amazing Grace', to name a few. These songs have endured and continue to bless and nourish the body of Christ many hundreds of years since they were written. They have outlived the hands that penned them and I am sure they will outlive the voices that are still singing them today.

I'm sure you could add some more modern examples of more recent worship choruses to the list, such as 'Shout To The Lord', 'The Heart of Worship', 'Light of The World', and '10, 000 Reasons (Bless The Lord)' and 'What a Beautiful Name', for example. They have an air of heaven about them and are sure to run the race till the end.

Songs are by no means the only area where lasting fruit can be produced. God wants us to produce it wherever we can, in every area of our life, culture and society. Fruit that will be an eternal stamp of heaven upon the earth. Fruit that will endure.

CHAPTER NINE

Live Your Song

The majority of songs that truly touch hearts and connect the heart of the worshipper, or listener, to God are songs born out of experience. A song's depth and meaning is often dug out from the experiences of life that the songwriter has had. Your life shines through your songs.

Songs Born out of Personal Experience

Personally, most of what I write starts with my experiences, then as a sort of therapeutic or reflective process I write them as songs. Keeping songs born out of experience helps to give the song guts. It keeps them grounded in a sense of reality rather than songs that are too idealistic and therefore run the risk of becoming 'out of reach' of those singing them. We also need to know what we are talking about. Once we have experienced the provision of God, or his forgiveness and mercy, for example, the songs we write should be birthed out of that experience and will therefore be more realistic. This will make them much more accessible to those singing them and enable the singer to take ownership of the song much more easily.

A beautiful aspect of writing congregational worship songs is the privilege of crafting and providing words that express different aspects of life and experience in such a way where the worshippers using the song can take ownership of it. A friend of mine once complimented my song writing ability by saying that he was grateful that I was able to write songs that put things into words that he felt he wanted to say to God, but did not know how to say them. This is a great honour, and a great responsibility.

The Experience of the Local Church

This is also true for the life of a church or congregation. Songs coming out of your local church also play a big part in reflecting and responding to the life of the church as a whole. If your church is going through a time of spiritual warfare, or is going through a time of lament, or is being captivated again by the wonder of the cross, for example, this should be reflected in the songs being sung. Songs born out of this unique and particular experience are invaluable to the life of the local church as they reflect its personal journey with God as well as provide a response back to God from the midst of the situation.

Be a F.A.T. Songwriter

An acronym that has stuck with me for many years is F.A.T. It stands for 'Faithful', 'Available' and 'Teachable'.

We are called to be faithful. We need to be faithful in living a life of purity and holiness, obedient to God in all we do. We need to be faithful in pursuing our relationship with God and cultivating our times of intimacy and worship with Him. We need to be faithful with our gifts and talents, to invest in them, develop and grow them and then use them to glorify the Lord. We also need to be faithful in the service of our local church, God's house. We need to be committed to its vision and be prepared to get involved and invest in it.

We are called to be available. We need to be ready to be used by God. To live our lives in such a way that we are walking in God's will and are eager to follow Him wherever He leads. We need to be available to take risks for God's glory, in the pursuit of the destiny he has set aside for us.

We are called to be teachable. To be prepared to work hard at investing in and improve our skills and talents for God's glory. To be willing to learn new things about God and about the gifts he has given us. To seek understanding and wisdom: "My son, if you accept my words and store up my commands within you, turning your ear to wisdom and applying your heart to understanding, and if you call out for insight and cry aloud for understanding, and if you look for it as for silver and search for it as for hidden treasure, then you will understand the fear of the Lord and find the knowledge of God. For the Lord gives wisdom and from his mouth come knowledge and understanding" (Proverbs 2:1-6, NIV).

Chill Out!

After reading a book like this, you could become pre-occupied with the 'mechanics' of song writing. I want to encourage you to relax and chill out! Don't get too stressed about not writing the 'perfect song' every time, or even writing a song at all! Song writing is a long process and takes a long time to develop. Don't be discouraged. Keep on pursuing your dreams. The thing that is even better than writing songs *for* God is to simply lose yourself in worship *of* Him. Remember, the best songs are birthed out of experience, so the more you experience God's presence, the more His presence will infuse the songs you write.

Be Yourself

As I have travelled along my personal journey as a songwriter I discover time and time again how important it is to be myself. There is a big temptation to try to write a song that sounds like the latest most popular song that is currently sweeping the globe – to imitate rather than to innovate.

Now don't get me wrong, you can learn things from popular songs, but don't try to duplicate them. Stay true to yourself and who God has called you to be. Just because you don't have three keyboard players, a whole strings and brass section and four people doing different electric guitar parts, it doesn't mean you can't write an awesome song. The key is to not to try to write a song that requires all sorts of things that you don't have. Use what's in your hand. Start where you are and be satisfied with your sound. Learn, develop, improve – by all means – but grow into the songwriter God is calling you to be, not a cheap imitation of someone else.

Be yourself – you are fearfully and wonderfully made by an almighty, all loving, all powerful God – a God who loves the sound he has made you to create and release!

CHAPTER TEN

And Finally

We have arrived at our destination after our short journey together. I hope you have enjoyed reading the ramblings of a fellow traveller and I am grateful that you have taken the time to invest in your talent.

We are living in exciting times. The kingdom of God is advancing and we are part of it. We have been entrusted with the awesome responsibility to craft songs of praise and worship that bless God's heart and encourage His people. So draw from the source of all creativity. Invest in your relationship with God. Get intimate with the lover of your soul. Use the gifts and talents that God has entrusted to you to bring Him glory.

Songcraft

Express the profound truth of His Word in a simple, yet fresh and dynamic way. Produce fruit that has enduring qualities that will take God's message forward to future generations as well as blessing the generation and culture that we live in now. Write songs that will enable others to draw ever closer to God in worship. Be bold and courageous. Take risks. Press on towards the destiny that God has for your life. But most of all, relax, and simply enjoy worshipping the Name that is above all names!

Useful Websites

I am aware that the nature of the Internet is such where things are always in a state of flux and change is inevitable. At the time of printing this book, the websites listed here exist.

www.uk.ccli.com

CCLI is a world leader in Church Copyright Licensing. Having your song registered with CCLI enables churches all around the world to legally use your songs, display or print the lyrics and much more. If your songs are used you get paid a royalty which CCLI collects on your behalf. In recent years it has become a bit more difficult for independent grassroots songwriters to sign up with CCLI, although I would still suggest having a conversation with them about your music. Notice needs to be given if you wish to stop your agreement with CCLI. Check your contracts to find out what length of time that is.

www.cdbaby.com

CDbaby is a US based platform that enables independent musicians from anywhere in the world to distribute their music digitally on a wide variety of platforms that include Spotify, Apple Music, Deezer, Amazon Music, Google Music and more. The songwriter retains their rights to the song and pays a one-off upfront fee for the distribution. CDbaby collects money from sales and takes a small percentage cut before passing the money on to you.

www.christiansongwriters.org

This is the home of the 'Christian Songwriter's Network' and contains loads of goodies especially for the Christian Songwriter. It provides the opportunity to find songwriting contests for Christian music, participation in their active forum and opportunities to get your music heard.

Useful Websites

www.homegrownworship.com

Homegrown Worship is a ground-breaking initiative that desires to give voice to the song of the local church. They help record and distribute worship music from a variety of genres and countries around the world to a global audience. Sharing a new song at least once a week Homegrown Worship is a growing platform that champions grassroots worship artists.

www.horusmusic.global

Horus is a UK based music digital distributor. They charge an annual fee but include unlimited releases, pre-order set up, barcodes and ISRC's, phone support, playlist pitching, YouTube & monetisation.

www.leadworship.com

This is Paul Baloche's website, so contains a lot of his songs and products. However, it does have a great 'thoughts on worship' section where there are many useful articles about songwriting.

www.mattmcchlery.com

This is my personal website that contains songs I have written, CDs, chord charts etc. There are also some helpful articles about songwriting and worship leading as well as other areas in which I minister, such as preaching and writing books.

www.resoundworship.com

Resound Worship are an amazing bunch of people. Not only do they produce very singable top-quality worship songs that they share through their website, they also invest in training songwriters in their local context. They make a very entertaining monthly podcast that comes packed with goodies for the aspiring and veteran songwriter alike and is well worth a listen. This is also backed up with an annual songwriting retreat as well as events throughout the year.

www.songsolutions.org

Song Solutions is a music publisher as well as offering a service to administer the copyright and royalty collection of other Music Publishers catalogue of songs. Not only do they work closely with CCLI, they also work with other royalty collection agencies such as PRS and CMPA. If your songs are being sung by other churches, there is a high chance that Song Solutions will take you on. They will then administer all copyright and royalty collections for your song catalogue giving you one point of reference for what can be a very complicated process. They charge a fee of 25% of royalties collected – so they only make money if you do. You pay an upfront fee for them to take on your catalogue initially. In return they do not take their cut until a threshold of earnings is reached. From that point your royalties

Useful Websites

pay them and you don't need to pay them again, adding new songs to your catalogue as often as you like. If you wish to stop using their services they require six months' notice.

www.tunecore.co.uk

TuneCore is another way you can distribute your music across a host of digital platforms around the world. There is an annual subscription to use this service but the trade off is you get to keep 100% of all your sales. TuneCore also provides other services such as Publishing, YouTube and Ringtones but all at additional cost.

www.weareworship.com

WeAreWorship is a 'global song resource by worship leaders for worship leaders'[16]. As well as having a great song search function and a huge database of well known worship songs, there are some other elements to the website that are not that obvious on first glance. The blog section is a fantastic wealth of information, advice and training for every member of the worship team. There are also a few blogs about songwriting in particular. If you create a free account you get the opportunity to download a free MP3 and chord chart once a month.

---

[16] As stated on the homepage of www.weareworship.com/uk on 18.07.2019

The best feature this website has for worship songwriters is SongShare. This is a space where you can share up to three of your own songs with the world for free. I strongly advice you read the Terms & Conditions before sharing your songs, but other than that, it is a great way to give your song wings.

www.worshipcentral.org

Worship Central is headed up by Tim Hughes and the team at Gas Street Church in Birmingham, UK. It is a fantastic resource for worship leaders, bands and Christian songwriters. It runs a series of workshops and training days around the world as well as having a downloadable course for the whole worship team. The website mostly points you in the direction of where you can access their various types of training.

www.worshipfuel.com

WorshipFuel is a website by the Church copyright licenser CCLI, so comes with the CCLI Top 100 chart which can be changed by country. However, there is plenty of material on this site about songwriting and I personally think the content on WorshipFuel is top-quality. There are also other articles and features that cover things like vocals, worship teams and gear.

Useful Websites

www.worshipsongrecording.com

Worship Song Recording exists to help the worship songwriter to record a professional version of their song. It is done from a distance, so you don't need to be in the UK to go to the studio. All you need is a rough demo of your song recorded on your phone or some basic recording software and a chord chart. You send this to them and they work their magic. There are a variety of pricing options available. Have a listen to their 'Audio Demos' to get an idea of what is possible.

Thanks

Thanks go to all the wonderful people in my life who have helped me along the way of this continuing songwriting adventure: Darren Beevers, who first encouraged my meagre efforts; Gareth Lowe, you inspire all around you; Andrew Baird, who never lets you get away with writing rubbish; Tim Hughes and Al Gordon, keep teaching and equipping the church lads; Ryan Baker-Barnes, here's to many more great songs we will write together Thanks also to Andy Baker, Nick Law and Loulita Gill from Homegrown Worship and Joel Payne and the team at Resound Worship for more recent encouragement and walking alongside me.

Songcraft

To all at the King's Church, Wisbech, thanks for your support and encouragement. Thanks for putting up with me and for singing my songs.

My lovely wife, Verity whose tireless patience, encouragement and support have helped me along the way. My amazing children: Katrina, Lara and Elijah. I love seeing who you are becoming and am privileged that God allowed me to be your Dad because I get to join in!

To those who've helped with this book: Patrick Johnstone, thanks for your insight, input and advice; Anna Smith, for proof reading the manuscript and for all your support; Al Gordon, Nick Law, Dave Bilbrough, Tommy and Jonny Deuschle, Loulita Gill and Michal Maddix-Hayford, for writing such fantastic endorsements; Geraldine Latty and Kat Mill for allowing me to use some of your thoughts and ideas; Chris Mercer and Andy Rogers, for your encouragement to write this book and to get it printed!

About The Author

Speaker, author, songwriter and worship leader, Matt McChlery was born in Zimbabwe. From an early age, it was apparent that he had natural musical ability. Shortly after his 13th birthday, at a 'Penguins In Africa' Christian rock concert, he committed his life to Jesus.

Following this, Matt started getting involved in his school youth group. With a little guidance, Matt taught himself how to play guitar and started facilitating worship at the age of 15. It was at Rhodes University, South Africa, where Matt's songwriting really started to show signs of maturity and were increasingly used to bless his local church.

Songwriting runs in the family as Matt's great, great, great grandfather, Rev. Sabine Baring-Gould wrote the classic hymn 'Onward Christian Soldiers'. Matt believes that some of the anointing he carries is part of a generational blessing as well as an individual mantle and calling upon his own life.

After recording his first single in 2002, Matt has won various awards for his music and blog and racking up airplay on hundreds of radio stations around the world as well as appearing on TV a few times.

In early 2016 Matt was diagnosed with cancer (non-Hodgkin's Lymphoma) so took some time out of performing and recording. However he continued to write his blog and chronicled his journey whilst battling the disease which has since become a source of insight and inspiration for thousands of people around the world. Later that year, shortly after finding out that he is now in full remission, his blog achieved 'Finalist' position in the Premier Digital Awards in the 'Most Inspiring Leadership Blog' category.

About the Author

Matt has written two books 'Songcraft' and 'All Things New: Stories of Transformed Lives' which have led to Matt adding speaking and preaching to his repertoire which have developed and come out of developments already happening within his ministry in his local church.

In 2019 Matt was one of the 10 'Handpicked' worship songwriters who teamed up with Homegrown Worship to release a new worship song every week. Matt personally contributed 4 songs to the project which were released through Homegrown Worship throughout 2019.

Matt lives with his wife Verity and their three children in the UK. In 2018 he took the decision to step away from being a Primary School teacher to purse full-time ministry. He has also started a small part-time tutoring business to help supplement his income.

He is an Overseer (Elder) at his local church, The King's Church, Wisbech, where he preaches, leads worship and is working on the strategic development of the church.

Let's Get Writing

Here are a few blank pages for you to use to write down your own song ideas, thoughts, inspirations and perhaps, even a finished song. Have fun.

Songcraft

Let's Get Writing

Songcraft

Let's Get Writing
For guitarists

Song: _____

Artist: _____

For pianists

Books
by Matt McChlery

Songcraft: Exploring the Art of Christian Songwriting

All Things New: Stories of Transformed Lives

Albums & EPs
by Matt McChlery

Fly

A Deeper Longing

All Things New

No One Like Jesus

Matt McChlery Ministries exists to Point People to Jesus.

Website: **www.mattmcchlery.com**

Email: **info@mattmcchlery.com**

Connect with Matt McChlery:

@mattmcchlery

@mattmcchlerymin

www.ingramcontent.com/pod-product-compliance
Lightning Source LLC
Chambersburg PA
CBHW070913080526
44589CB00013B/1273